HERBS

MICHAEL JANULEWICZ

HarperCollinsPublishers

Editor Emma Johnson
Designers James Marks, Steve Wilson
Picture research Moira McIlroy

First published 1988 by
HarperCollins Publishers

This edition published 1992

A CIP catalogue record for this book is available from the British Library.

Photoset by Bookworm Typesetting
Printed and bound in Hong Kong by Dai Nippon Printing Company

Front cover: Melissa, chives, purple sage by The Harry Smith Horticultural Photographic Collection
Back cover: Iden Croft garden by Lyn and Derek Gould

CONTENTS

INTRODUCTION

Herbs are our oldest garden plants and for centuries they have provided flavouring for the cook, medicines for the physician, cosmetics, dyes and perfumes. For today's gardener they are equally rewarding and the great variety of form, foliage, and flowers that they offer makes them useful in most parts of the garden.

Herb garden, Sissinghurst

GROWING HERBS

The majority of garden herbs grow wild along the coasts of the Mediterranean and the hot dry summers and relatively mild winters of their native habitat provide a clue to their successful cultivation. With few exceptions, herbs need a sunny position and a well-drained soil with a pH value between 6.0 and 7.5. A prolonged wet winter spell will be disastrous for their root system. Without ideal growing conditions – even if they are good-natured enough to survive – herbs will grow thin and drawn and lose much of their fragrance and flavour.

Herbs for shade There are exceptions to the general rule. Some woodland herbs require shade, while others will tolerate partial shade (see list below).

Planning your herb garden The ideal position for a herb bed is in a south-facing part of the garden. But few gardeners are blessed with a southern aspect, so as a general rule ensure that the herb garden receives at least five hours of sun each day.

When you have established a suitable site it is time to consider the shape and size of the new bed. In the majority of gardens the most practical shape is rectangular, but for anyone with plenty of space, other design ideas can be found on pages 12-17.

Whatever design you choose, always remember that a herb garden must be practical. A bed that is too wide will not allow you to pick the herbs that grow at the back, or means you will have to trample down the plants at the front to reach them. If you have access from one side only, then the bed should be no wider than 1m (3ft), while access from both sides should enable you to extend the width to 1.5m (5ft). As for size, there is no need to be over-

Herbs that tolerate partial shade

- Angelica
- Anise hyssop
- Bergamot
- Catmint
- Chives
- Comfrey
- Elecampane
- Horehound
- Hyssop
- Lady's mantle
- Lovage
- Mint
- Pennyroyal
- Sorrel
- Sweet cicely
- Woad
- Woodruff
- Wormwood

ambitious – a 2m (6ft) long bed is sufficient to begin with and can always be added to as your herb collection grows.

Preparing the soil Herbs thrive in a loose, well-drained soil that includes a certain amount of organic material. Add about a third in bulk of well-rotted compost or moss peat to loosen up heavy clay soils, or add nutrient-holding bulk to sandy soils. Also check the chemistry of the soil – the aim is to create a neutral soil of about pH 6.0 to 7.5. Use a soil-testing kit to determine the acidity or alkalinity and, if necessary, correct the pH by adding proprietary compounds that are available at most garden centres.

Drainage If the site you have chosen is badly drained then you have problems. These can be solved in two ways – by installing a drainage layer or building a raised bed. To make a drainage layer dig out the bed to a depth of 30cm (1ft), keeping the top-soil and sub-soil in separate heaps. Line the bottom of the bed with gravel, stones or rubble to a depth of 7.5cm (3in). Replace the sub-soil and then the top-soil and rake to a fine tilth.

Building a raised bed The use of raised beds is a tradition in herb gardening. It ensures the drainage that most herbs need, and the raised soil warms up quicker in spring to allow annuals to be sown or planted earlier in the year. They also keep the garden neat and accentuate the formal pattern of the planting. In addition, they make harvesting easier as there is less distance to bend when picking leaves or flowers.

A raised bed is particularly suitable close to a patio or sitting area where the strong scents can be more easily appreciated.

Almost any kind of material can be used for edging the bed. Stone and bricks provide a rot-proof edging, but timber will need to be coated with a preservative. However, never use creosote as this is toxic to all plants.

Checking drainage To check the drainage in the site you have chosen, dig a hole 30cm (1ft) wide and 30cm (1ft) deep. Fill it with water. If water is left in the hole an hour later then the drainage is inadequate for the herb bed.

Checklist

Make sure that the bed:
1 receives 5 hours sun a day
2 is well-drained
3 is neither too acid nor too alkaline
4 is of a size that allows you to reach all of the herbs easily

CARE AND PROPAGATION

Given the correct growth conditions, herbs need relatively little care. They are mostly resistant to pests and diseases as the oils they contain act as repellents. However, some of the soft-leaved plants can fall prey to leaf-chewing insects and aphids. You can either live with the loss, remove the offending pest mechanically (by hand or by spraying with water from a hose) or you can use a proprietary insecticide such as 'Picket' up to the day of picking.

Good garden hygiene is the best prevention. Remove dead or dying leaves and stems and put them on the bonfire. In autumn, when the leaves of perennials have died, cut the old stalks down to ground level and, along with the dead leaves and stems of annuals, add them to the compost heap.

Weeding Always keep the herb bed free of weeds. This not only reduces the competition for moisture and nutrients, but also keeps the bed visually tidy. This is particularly important if you have created a formal design for the bed. A summer mulch of 'Forest Bark' Chipped Bark spread 5cm (2in) deep will keep most weeds out and also help to retain moisture in the soil.

If the bed is unprotected during heavy winter frosts, then move bay trees and rosemary bushes indoors.

Propagation Most herbs are available pot-grown from nurseries and garden centres, but it is cheaper, and more fun, to propagate your own – either from your own stock or from that of a friend or neighbour. Herbs can be propagated either by seed, root division or by cutting.

Sowing seeds All annuals and biennials, and most perennials, can be raised from seed. The instructions on the seed packet will provide all the information you need, but as a general rule sow seeds in spring as soon as the ground is suitable, and cover with soil to about three times their diameter. Seeds can be sown in rows, or in patches if used in a mixed border or herb garden. Water the seeds with a fine spray and ensure that the soil is moist but not waterlogged. Always mark where you have sown seeds as they will not be

1

2

Many herbs can be propagated from stem cuttings, like lavender, rosemary, lemon balm and wormwood. Use young shoots about 10cm (4in) long, cutting just below a leaf joint (1). Strip off lower leaves. Insert in pots of cutting compost – equal parts peat and sand (2).

1. Clump and mat forming plants like chives can be divided in spring.

2. Lift the clumps, pull them apart, into small pieces, and immediately replant.

3. Woody herbs like bay can be propagated from heel cuttings by pulling off shoots.

4. The heel is trimmed cleanly with a knife before inserting the cutting.

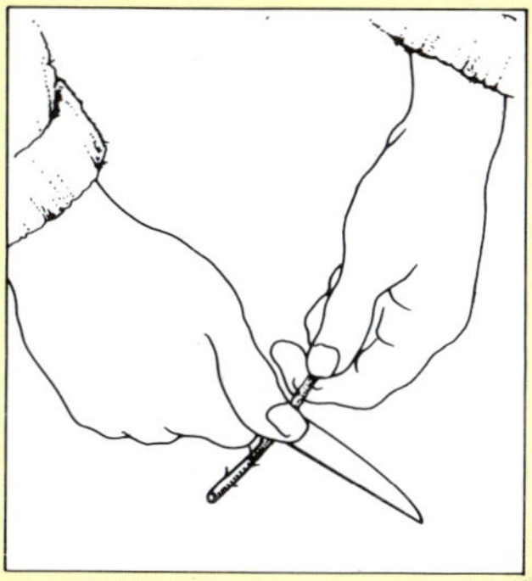

5. Bergamot, comfrey and some other herbs can be increased from root cuttings.

6. Cut roots into 5cm (2in) pieces in autumn and insert in pots of sandy compost.

recognisable until they have germinated and produced their first true leaves.

Sowing seeds in pots or containers indoors has the advantage of extending the growing season and is particularly useful for slow-growing perennials such as winter savory and for half-hardy annuals such as basil, which needs plenty of warmth to germinate. Use a proprietary potting compost and sow the seeds about a month before the last frost is expected. Dampen the soil in the container a little before sowing. Cover the pot with plastic to hold the moisture and increase humidity until the seeds have germinated. Then remove the covering and place them on a windowsill, remembering to turn them each day so they do not become distorted stretching for the light. Do not allow the seedlings to become too crowded; when they are large enough to handle transfer them to other containers or thin them with scissors, leaving the strongest ones to grow.

HERBS FOR THE KITCHEN

Although herbs can be grown in odd corners of the garden among other plants, or in a corner of a kitchen garden, it is both pleasant and practical to have them growing together in a bed near the kitchen where they are close to hand. The herbs most used in cooking – although by no means the only ones – are basil, bay, chives, marjoram, mint, parsley, rosemary, sage, tarragon and thyme. These ten herbs should provide all your culinary needs to begin with. All are easy to grow, but continuity of supply can be difficult to arrange and it is necessary to make special efforts if this is the aim of the cook/gardener.

Unfortunately, for garden planning, parsley and mint are moisture-lovers, and can be difficult to please in the dry sunny conditions needed by the other plants. Unless the herb bed provides some shade and a damp root run, it is probably best to tuck them away from the rest in another part of the garden. Continuous cropping may also make the plants look untidy, and fairly large patches are needed to ensure a continued supply to the kitchen.

Parsley needs to be sown twice to keep enough for regular cropping – April and August sowings should

TEN COMMON KITCHEN HERBS

NAME	DESCRIPTION
Basil *Ocimum basilicum*	hardy annual, bright green leaves which can be used fresh or dried; 60-90cm (2-3ft)
Bay (sweet bay) *Laurus nobilis*	hardy evergreen shrub with glossy aromatic leaves; thrives in seaside gardens; 3-5.5m (10-18ft)
Chives *Allium schoenoprasum*	herbaceous perennial; grass-like hollow leaves which have an onion flavour; 15-25cm (6-10in)
Marjoram (pot) *Origanum onites*	herbaceous perennial; bright green aromatic leaves and pinkish flowers; use leaves fresh or dried; 30cm (12in)
Mint *Mentha*	herbaceous perennial; common types for cooking are applemint, spearmint and peppermint; 60-90cm (2-3ft)
Parsley *Petroselinum crispum*	biennial; produces a mass of curly leaves that have a wide range of uses; 30-60cm (12-24in)
Rosemary *Rosmarinus officinalis*	shrub with thin narrow leaves growing densely on each stem, small attractive purple flowers; 1.8-2.1m (6-7ft)
Sage *Salvia officinalis*	shrub with pale grey-green leaves with a strong aromatic scent when crushed; 60cm (2ft)
Tarragon *Artemesia dracunculus*	herbaceous perennial; grey-green narrow leaves; pick them when they are young, use fresh or dried; 45-60cm (1½-2ft)
Thyme *Thymus vulgaris*	shrub with mid to dark green leaves, or gold-leaved form 'Aureus'; pungently flavoured; purple flowers; 10-20cm (4-8in)

provide enough cover for the seasons – and the annual basil should be sown in early spring indoors or under glass and transferred to the garden as soon as the danger of frost has passed.

Mint can be a problem in a small bed as its invasive roots will soon run wild and take over the bed. It is best, therefore, to grow mint in pots or a bottomless bucket plunged into the soil up to the rim. An added advantage with a pot is that it can be brought indoors during February to provide fresh shoots a month or so later.

The remaining kitchen herbs will fit into a sunny bed about 2m × 2m (6ft × 6ft). A single bush of sage will suffice – if happy it will grow to 1m (3ft) across within a few years. Marjoram and chives die down each winter, but their cropping life can be extended by taking a few roots indoors in autumn (see pages 18-19).

Thyme, like sage, becomes straggly in about three or four years and the plants will need to be replaced.

Rosemary and bay are more permanent features. Rosemary will grow gradually into a handsome bush, although some varieties sprawl considerably and overcrowd neighbours. The compact upright variety 'Miss Jessups' will keep its shape well in a small plot and can be clipped to keep it in bounds. Bay also responds to clipping and can be trained to a convenient size.

LEFT The ten herbs shown in the chart will supply most of the needs of the kitchen; the more adventurous cook may wish to increase the range of culinary herbs grown in the garden.

RIGHT The list gives a range of herbs to complement a particular type of food. The culinary uses of all herbs are included in the descriptions on pages 22-47.

HERBS TO USE WITH CERTAIN FOODS

SOUPS	Basil, bay, chervil, chives, coriander, dill, lovage, marjoram, parsley, sage, savory, sweet cicely, tarragon, thyme.
BREADS	Basil, coriander, dill, fennel, marjoram, parsley, savory, thyme.
FISH	Basil, bay, dill, lemon balm, lovage, marjoram, rosemary, sage, savory, tarragon, thyme.
EGGS	Basil, bay, chervil, chives, dill, fennel, garlic, marjoram, parsley, rosemary, savory, tarragon, thyme.
SHELL-FISH	Basil, bay, dill, lemon balm, marjoram, savory, tarragon, thyme.
POULTRY	Basil, bay, dill, lemon balm, lovage, marjoram, parsley, rosemary, sage, savory, tarragon, thyme.
LAMB	Basil, bay, dill, garlic, marjoram, mint, rosemary, sage, savory, tarragon, thyme.
BEEF	Basil, bay, chervil, dill, garlic, marjoram, parsley, rosemary, sage, savory, tarragon, thyme.
PORK	Basil, coriander, dill, fennel, marjoram, rosemary, sage, tarragon, thyme.
VEGETABLES	Basil, bay, chervil, coriander, dandelion, dill, lovage, marjoram, mint, parsley, rosemary, sage, savory, sweet cicely, salad burnet, tarragon, thyme.
CHEESES	Basil, chervil, chives, coriander, dill, mint, nasturtium, sage, tarragon, thyme.
DESSERTS	Bay, coriander, marigold, thyme, sweet cicely, lemon verbena

THE FORMAL HERB GARDEN

The first herb gardens in monasteries and castle courtyards were strictly functional. They were laid out with small, rather empty rectangular beds with plenty of walking and picking space between them. The garden was often enclosed to protect the plants from wind and frost and for reasons of security. This tradition of enclosure and formal planting continues today and still forms the perfect formula for herb garden design.

While few gardeners have the space for planning a formal garden enclosed by hedges, dividing the area set aside for herbs into small rectangular plots and arranging the planting in a complementary way, will give a charming traditional look to the garden. Fortunately, herbs associate well with paving, stone or bricks. A careful, but not fussy, combination of materials can provide just the right setting. The balance of formality and informality can be organized by the amount of plant-growth that is permitted to spill over to soften the edges, or by the controlled use of creeping thyme or chamomile in the cracks between the hard materials. Neither plant will object to being trodden on.

The Elizabethan knot garden
With the dissolution of the monasteries by Henry VIII in the middle of the sixteenth century, and the building of large, comfortable houses, the form of the herb garden changed. It was now meant to be viewed from the first floor windows of the new house, or from the terraces that surrounded it, and the formal pattern became more complex. This change of viewpoint popularized what is known as the knot garden.

In its simplest form the knot garden was designed as a wheel, the spokes being constructed of compact bulky herbs such as hyssop, rue and thyme and the segments being filled with shorter herbs. The hub would become a focal point, perhaps filled

A most attractive way of making a herb garden is to lay paving slabs in a checkerboard formation. The spaces between them consist of soil and are used for planting the herbs. This allows easy access to the herbs, even in wet weather.

by a clipped bay tree, a sundial or statue. Gradually the designs for knot gardens took on the form of complicated scroll patterns made of curves and lines of miniature box or lavender hedges. The spaces were filled with herbs, ornamental flowers such as pinks and marigolds, or even coloured gravel.

Making a knot garden A knot garden can be built on quite a small scale, with beds divided by low hedges or gravel on a site perhaps only 3m × 3m (10ft × 10ft).

Choose a sunny level site, ideally one that can be viewed from above. Plan the knot on paper first, using a pair of compasses to create the pattern of circle, square and arcs. When you come to apply the design to the garden you can mark the pattern on the site using sand from an upturned bottle that is attached to a stake.

RIGHT The traditional way of growing herbs is in a formal Elizabethan knot garden. The beds are edged with dwarf edging box and paths are formed with gravel. The knot garden is suited to a small area and any pattern can be created, the simplest being the wheel, with 'spokes' radiating from a central hub.

INFORMAL HERB GARDENING

When making an informal border it is important to plan the arrangement of the herbs before you begin to plant. Besides the growing conditions required by each plant, there are other important details to be taken into consideration, both practical and aesthetic.

Check the individual growth characteristics of each herb – height, spread, flowering time – and plan accordingly. Tall subjects such as angelica, fennel and tarragon should be planted at the back of the border so that they do not overshadow and obscure lower-growing herbs. Allow room for the plants to spread, as fast-growing plants such as thyme and pennyroyal will develop from one small plant to cover a fairly wide area within one growing season.

Herbs such as basil and parsley, that are to be gathered regularly, must be planted where they can be easily reached and in generous patches, if they are not to look untidy. For the same reason, plant good wide clumps of wispier annuals such as summer savory, caraway and coriander. Remember, too, to keep annuals and perennials separate – you do not want to be treading on the perennials while you are sowing the annuals.

The high season effect you should be aiming for is one of billowing luxuriant growth, with no soil showing, but in a controlled and intentional fashion. Contrast of foliage is also important to give the bed some interest, and here the dark green evergreens such as bay provide a useful contrast to the ferny foliage of fennel and dill and the solid grey mounds of cotton lavender.

Grey-leaved plants can be used on their own to create a silver garden in which the soft colouring and contrasting textures of the leaves create a delightful and unusual effect. Cotton lavender, silver-leaved thyme, sage, lavender and the curry plant provide a variety of heights and leaves that blend together into a softly aromatic border.

ABOVE Some herbs are grown for their attractive foliage, including grey-leaved rue and the golden sage.

RIGHT The neat, low-growing golden marjoram makes a most attractive edging for a flower border.

Herbs for every corner If you have no room for a planned herb garden this does not mean that you cannot grow herbs. Indeed, many herbs are attractive additions to any flower border and can be grown solely for their flowers or foliage. Such plants as angelica, fennel, lemon balm, sweet cicely, marigolds, rue and valerian have much to offer the flower gardener.

Some plants are useful as edging – lavender, cotton lavender, sage and rosemary, for example, can be clipped into small hedges. The rock garden can also find a place for low-growing creeping perennials such as thyme, chamomile and pennyroyal and these also provide a good service in filling cracks in paths and drives, or helping to disguise the unsightly edges around drains and manhole covers. They provide a bonus by releasing a strong scent when trodden on. Similarly aromatic herbs, allowed to spill over onto the lawn, bring some pleasant relief to the chore of cutting the grass. Make sure, however, that any herbs you grow are approachable. There is no point in growing such aromatic herbs as lemon verbena or anise hyssop, whose leaves need to be crushed for you to enjoy their aroma, if you cannot reach them. In old country gardens bushes of rosemary could be found near the entrance gate where they could be smelled and picked and washing could be spread on the bushes for airing.

Several herbs seem particularly enjoyable in the burst of sun following rain, so it is best if they are planted near a path or paved area if they are to be enjoyed to the full.

SPECIAL HERB COLLECTIONS

The long history and varied uses of herbs provide a rich source of ideas for special collections or themes for the herb garden. Some people choose to grow every herb mentioned in the Bible or the works of William Shakespeare, others to re-create a particular historic garden, others to make a scented garden ... the variety of different themes is limited only by imagination. Some ideas are given below.

A bee garden At one time honey was the only sweetener available and herbs that attracted bees were highly valued. Some, such as savory and rosemary, actually added flavour to the honey.

A scented garden Strong scents add a certain magical quality to the garden. Flowers such as roses, lilies, honeysuckle and jasmine will all add their fragrance to the garden. Herbs, with their variety of form, colour, foliage and flowers, as well as their delicate scent, are essential elements.

A tea garden Herb teas, or tisanes, have been enjoyed for centuries, both as refreshing drinks and as aids to digestion. Many are still used by homeopaths for medicinal reasons. Teas made with the dried herbs need one teaspoon for each cup and another for the pot, fresh herbs need three teaspoons per cup.

Make the tea in the usual way, allowing it to brew for five to ten minutes. For teas made with the seeds of herbs such as dill, fennel and lovage, the seeds must be pounded in a mortar first. Then simmer in boiling water for five to ten minutes.

Herbs for a bee garden

- Anise hyssop
- Bergamot
- Borage
- Catmint
- Horehound
- Hyssop
- Rosemary
- Savory
- Sweet cicely

Sweet cicely (right), Rosemary and rue (opposite, top), Sages, purple and variegata (opposite, bottom).

Herbs for a scented garden

- Angelica
- Anise
- Basil
- Bay
- Bergamot
- Catmint
- Chamomile
- Clary
- Costmary
- Cotton lavender
- Cumin
- Fennel
- Fenugreek
- Horehound
- Hyssop
- Lavender
- Lemon balm
- Lemon thyme
- Mints
- Pennyroyal
- Rosemary
- Rue
- Southernwood
- Sweet cicely
- Valerian
- Woodruff

The most common herb teas are made from the leaves and flowers of

- Angelica
- Basil
- Bergamot
- Borage
- Chamomile
- Catmint
- Horehound
- Hyssop
- Lemon balm
- Lemon verbena
- Lovage
- Meadowsweet
- Mint
- Parsley
- Rosemary
- Sage
- Salad burnet
- Thyme
- Vervain
- Woodruff

Medicinal herbs At one time the use of herbs in medicine was second only to their culinary use. Many of the herbal cures now seem rather fanciful, but before the advent of modern drugs the tried and tested cures derived from herbs were all that existed. Herbal medicine has never disappeared and there is a modern trend to hark back to the old remedies and 'natural' cures.

Making your own medicines can be a somewhat hazardous occupation because many of the herbs have dangerous and unexpected side-effects. In this book we have not listed the medicinal qualities of herbs because they cannot be vouched for in all cases. If you are interested in growing and using medicinal herbs, it is wise to investigate the stock of your nearest herbal or homeopathic supplier first.

GROWING HERBS INDOORS

Herbs make attractive, aromatic and useful houseplants, and for people without gardens a selection grown in pots indoors or in a window box on a sunny window-sill will keep the kitchen supplied for most of the year. Growing indoors has the added advantage of prolonging the season of annual herbs such as basil and summer savory.

Larger herbs, such as borage, fennel and sage will grow happily in pots, but will always be smaller than when they are grown in the garden. Beware of herbs with extensive and invasive root systems such as tarragon, lemon balm and all varieties of mint as they will soon overrun their neighbours in a window box. Keep them in pots and plunge them into the window box soil.

Where to grow Herbs grown indoors need plenty of sun and light. South- or west-facing windows are generally best, but remember the sun-lovers such as thyme should be next to the window while the mints will prefer semi-shade. Turn pots by 45 degrees each day to ensure that the plant grows evenly and does not become drawn as it stretches for the light.

No herb likes a sudden change of temperature, so the kitchen is not usually the best room to site them. A coolish room that never exceeds 16°C (61°F) by day and never drops below 10°C (50°F) by night, is ideal.

Soil Proprietary brands of herb potting compost can be obtained from most garden centres and horticultural suppliers, but if you want to make your own, a mixture of equal parts of sand, leaf mould and ordinary garden soil will be adequate. Fill the pots to within 2.5cm (1in) of the rim. Bay trees, which are traditionally grown in pots, will need a richer potting mixture.

Herbs to grow in pots and window boxes

The best plants for this purpose are those with a low-growing habit. A good selection is:

basil	marjoram
chervil	parsley
chives	thyme

Planting If you want quick results it is probably best to buy small plants, but it is quite simple to propagate your own from seed or cuttings. Methods of propagation are given on pages 8-9. To make propagating even simpler it is now possible to buy boxes or pots of ready-to-germinate seeds.

Caring for herbs in pots The rules for growing herbs indoors are the same as for most houseplants. Keep them well-ventilated but away from draughts, feed them with liquid fertilizer, do not allow them to dry out and, most importantly, do not overwater – a waterlogged soil will quickly kill the roots. When the roots begin to protrude through the drainage hole of the pot it is time to repot the plant.

Harvesting Never remove more than one-fifth of the leaves of the plant at any one time, and wait for new leaf-growth to appear before cropping again. Chives, however, may have all their leaves cut at one harvest, but if you want a continual supply grow two or three plants.

Many herbs can be grown indoors on a light sunny window-sill, but be careful in your choice. The large vigorous herbs like fennel are better in pots to keep them small, while less-invasive kinds are more suited to a window box.

HARVESTING AND STORING

The aroma and flavour of herbs is contained in volatile oils that are found in very small glands in the leaves and stems, or inside narrow canals within the leaves and fruits. The art of preserving herbs is to retain as much of these oils as possible.

Harvesting Always gather herbs in early morning, just after the dew has evaporated and before the sun has had a chance to evaporate the volatile oils. Never pick herbs if they are damp after rain. Points to remember when harvesting herbs are: use a sharp knife and avoid handling to reduce the possibility of bruising; only collect the amount you can deal with quickly – herbs left lying around for any length of time soon lose their flavour; keep different herbs separate to avoid cross-flavouring and label each batch; and dispose of any browned or damaged leaves or flowers.

Drying Like all plants, herbs contain about 70 per cent water. The art of successful drying is to remove the water quickly without losing the oils. The best drying conditions found are in a dark, well-ventilated place at a temperature of between 21°C (70°F) and 38°C (100°F).

Too much light can destroy the colouring and the ventilation is important to carry away the humidity created by the drying plants.

An airing cupboard, the plate-warming part of an oven, or even a darkened room with a small fan-heater are all good places to choose, and the herbs should be fully dried

RIGHT Herbs are best gathered when the leaves are dry and before the sun has evaporated the volatile oils.
FAR RIGHT Dry herbs as quickly as possible in a high temperature, and in darkness to prevent loss of colour.

in 4-14 days. Place the herbs, one layer deep, on flat trays, preferably ones that allow circulation of air through perforations in their bases. Muslin, hessian or any open-weave cloth stretched over a wooden frame is ideal.

Bunches of herbs hung up in the kitchen look attractive, but this method will retain less flavour as the herbs will take up to three weeks to dry fully. Leaves are dry when they are brittle, petals when they feel dry and slightly crisp.

Storing Strip leaves from the stems and crumble them before putting them into air-tight containers. Do not grind them too finely or they will lose their flavour more quickly. Herbs such as rosemary, sage and thyme can be left on the stalk. This makes it easier to remove them from stew or roast meat dishes. Keep dried bay leaves whole. Place seeds and flowers in air-tight containers as soon as they are dry.

Always keep dried herbs in glass jars, never plastic or paper containers. Paper will absorb the oils and plastic tends to make the herbs 'sweat'. If moisture does begin to form on the inside of the glass container, the herbs have not been completely dried. Remove them and lay them on some paper to allow them to dry further.

How long will dried herbs last? Most will last for about a year, although basil, lovage, mint and marjoram will last longer. However, lemon balm, parsley, summer savory and tarragon only last for nine months. Try to replace all dried herbs each year. Dating the containers when you fill them will help you to keep track of the length of time that you have kept them.

Freezing Some herbs lose their flavour when dried and it is best to use them fresh. Freezing is particularly suitable for soft-leaved herbs.

When you have collected the herbs, wash them if they are dusty and shake them dry. They can be frozen as they are if you want to use them within two months, but for longer storage tie them into bunches, dip each bunch into boiling water and then into chilled water to blanch them. Pack in foil or plastic bags, seal and freeze. Frozen herbs can be frozen for about six months.

Herbs that freeze well:
- Basil
- Chervil
- Chives
- Dill
- Fennel
- Mint
- Marjoram
- Parsley
- Sorrel

SIXTY OF THE BEST HERBS

Herbs can be grown for a variety of reasons; you may wish to create a scented garden, keep the kitchen supplied with culinary herbs or provide an aromatic ground cover along the sides of a patio area. The 60 herbs described here should fulfil your needs and help you to make your choice. Each entry describes the growth habit of each herb, where it will grow, how to propagate it, when to harvest it and how to use it. The *Herb garden planner* on pages 46-7 summarizes all this essential information in one useful chart.

ANGELICA

Angelica archangelica
One of the tallest and most decorative of herbs, reaching a height of 2m (6ft). It will tolerate semi-shade but requires a fairly rich soil and ample moisture. Angelica is a biennial and dies once it has flowered, but it can be kept as a semi-perennial if the flowers are removed before they open. It self-sows freely, but can be propagated by sowing seed in late summer, or by root division.
Harvesting Cut leaves as required during early summer. The stems should be harvested before the plant flowers.
Uses The leaves, fresh or dried, can be infused in boiling water for a tisane. The stems can be candied and used for cake decorations and to flavour jams.

ANISE

Pimpinella anisum
A 60cm (2ft) tall annual with serrated leaves and clusters of white flowers. Anise prefers a light dry and limy soil and needs a sheltered, sunny position. Sow seeds in spring when danger of frost has passed and thin plants to 20cm (8in) apart when they are large enough to handle. The fruits will only ripen in a hot summer.
Harvesting When the fruits have turned greyish-green cut the whole flower stem and hang upside down in an airy place to finish ripening. Shake out the seeds and store.
Uses The seeds are used to flavour biscuits, bread and cakes. They are also the basis of the flavouring of such drinks as Pernod, Ouzo and Arrak.

ANISE HYSSOP

Agastache foeniculum
A hardy perennial that grows to

Angelica

Anise hyssop

Basil

Bay

90cm (3ft) tall with spikes of purple flowers in mid-summer. Anise hyssop is happy in almost any soil, will tolerate light shade and prefers sunny but cool weather. Sow seeds in autumn for flowering in two years.
Harvesting Pick fresh leaves as required or for drying before the flowers have opened.
Uses Mainly ornamental but the aniseed-flavoured leaves, fresh or dried, can be used to make a tisane.

BASIL

Ocimum basilicum

A half-hardy annual that in good warm conditions will grow to about 30cm (1ft) high. It is a delicate plant and is best grown under glass. If you do not have a greenhouse, find the sunniest spot in the garden, or grow it in a pot on a sunny window-sill. Sow seeds in early spring. Pinching out the flowers prolongs the growth of fresh leaves.
Harvesting Cut leaves as required. The flavour changes when the leaves are dried.
Uses Goes well with tomato and egg dishes and almost all Italian food.

BAY

Laurus nobilis

A mature tree may grow to more than 3.5m (12ft) over 20 years. It bears small yellow flowers in spring, followed by purplish berries in a warm dry summer. Bay can be grown from seed sown in spring, but it is best to buy a small pot plant. Protect from frost in winter. Bay is an ideal plant for growing in tubs or large pots on a shaded balcony or patio and can be clipped to shape.
Harvesting Pick fresh leaves as required. Leaves should be dried in the dark to retain their colour.
Uses Marinades, pâtés, meat and fish stocks, soups and stews.

Bergamot

Borage

BERGAMOT
Monarda didyma
A decorative and fragrant perennial that grows to a height of 90cm (3ft). The honeysuckle-like flowers range in colour from white to pink, purple and red. Bergamot enjoys moisture and will tolerate semi-shade. Seeds sown in summer will germinate easily, or propagate by root division in spring or cuttings in autumn.
Harvesting Pick leaves or flowers as required. Dry in the dark to preserve colour.
Uses Leaves and flowers can be chopped and used in salads or with pork dishes. Its most common use is as a tea, known as Oswego tea, that is traditionally drunk by the North American Oswego Indians.

BORAGE
Borago officinalis
A sturdy annual that grows to a height of 60-90cm (2-3ft) with hairy stems and leaves and vivid blue flowers. Sow seeds in a sunny position in spring, spacing them 45cm (18in) apart. The plants reach maturity in five to six weeks. Once established, borage will sow itself freely.
Harvesting Use fresh leaves and flowers as required.
Uses The faint cucumber-like taste of the leaves are used in salads, or as flavourings to wine cups, such as Pimms, or with apple juice. The flowers can be candied and used for cake decorations.

CARAWAY
Carum carvi
A biennial which grows to about 60cm (2ft) in height. Caraway has delicate ferny leaves and umbels of white flowers. The flowers produce the caraway seeds that are harvested. Sow seeds in a sunny position in spring and thin them to

Caraway

23cm (9in) apart. Prune the plants in autumn and they will flower and seed the following summer. Once established caraway will seed itself.
Harvesting When the seeds are ripe, cut off the plants at ground level and hang up the sheaves in a dry airy place. When seeds are dry they can be shaken on to paper and stored in airtight jars.
Uses Cook the seeds in seed cakes and with fatty meats such as pork or goose, and especially with cabbage, carrots and cheese dishes. The fresh leaves can be added to salads.

CATMINT

Nepeta cataria
A hardy perennial that grows to a height of 90cm (3ft). Catmint grows in sun or partial shade and prefers light but well-composted soil. Sow seeds in spring or propagate by root division from late-autumn to early-spring. Prune catmint to keep a bushy shape.
Harvesting Pick leaves for use or drying as required.
Uses Catmint can be used to make tisanes or to flavour meats and salads. However, the only real reason to grow catmint is to excite and give pleasure to a pet cat. Strangely, some cats will not be affected, others will be thrown into an uncontrollable frenzy.

CHAMOMILE

There are two kinds of chamomile:
True chamomile
Matricarcia chamomilla
An annual that enjoys full sun and dry soils. Sow seeds in rows 23cm (9in) apart in spring.
Harvesting Pick flowers as they come into bloom and dry them in a dark airing cupboard.
Uses Appropriate for use in cosmetics, hair rinses for blonde hair and as a tisane.

Roman chamomile
Anthemis nobilis
This is the chamomile that is used to make lawns. Once planted it needs very little care.

CHERVIL

Anthriscus cerefolium
Similar in appearance to parsley, but more delicate, chervil has pale green fern-like leaves and small white flowers. It reaches a height of 60cm (2ft). Chervil prefers a light, well-drained but moist soil and needs semi-shade in mid-summer and full sun in spring and autumn. Although an annual, fresh chervil can be harvested for most of the year by successional sowing. Sow seed from early spring onwards in drills 30cm (12in) apart. Thin the seedlings to 20cm (5in). Plants will take about four weeks to reach maturity. To prevent them running to seed too quickly, pick off any flowers as they appear.
Harvesting Pick leaves about six weeks after sowing and before the flowers open.
Uses The leaves have a slight flavour of aniseed and should be used generously.

CHIVES

Allium schoenoprasum
Botanically, the chive plant is not a herb, but it is grown in the garden and used in the kitchen as one. Chives are a member of the onion family and produce clumps of green spear-like leaves about 25cm (10in) in height, with heads of purple-pink flowers in summer. They prefer a moist, slightly alkaline soil and semi-shade. Sow seeds in spring or early summer in drills 30cm (12in) apart and thin seedlings to 15cm (6in) apart. Every three or four years divide the plants into six or more bulbils and replant.

Chives

Harvesting Cut the leaves with scissors as required, about 2.5cm (1in) from ground level.
Uses In cooking, use anywhere a subtle onion flavour is required.

CLARY

Salvia sclarea
Clary is a biennial relative of sage, often grown as an annual. It has hairy heart-shaped leaves, spikes of pink and mauve flowers and reaches a height of 1m (3ft). Sow seeds in either spring or autumn in a sunny well-drained position.
Harvesting Pick fresh leaves as required and leaves for drying or freezing just before the flowers open.
Uses Clary can be used wherever sage would be added, or in wine cups and fruit drinks.

Clary

COMFREY

Symphytum officinale

The biggest and tallest of the borage family, comfrey is a perennial that reaches 1.2m (4ft) in height. The stem and leaves are hairy and the flowers may be coloured blue, purple, pink or white. Sow seeds in spring in a shady moist position or propagate by root cuttings in autumn. Comfrey self-seeds freely and can spread extremely quickly through a garden, so it may be wise to pinch out flower buds before they seed.

Harvesting Pick leaves as required

Uses Mainly decorative, but the leaves can be cooked like spinach or chopped fresh to be added to salads.

CORIANDER

Coriandrum sativum

An attractive feathery annual that grows to about 45cm (1½ft) in height and provides both leaves – with a flavour similar to dried orange-peel – and seeds for the kitchen. Sow the seeds in rich light soil in rows 30cm (1ft) apart throughout summer to provide a continuous supply of young leaves and a crop of seed.

Harvesting Pick young leaves as required. Seeds should not be harvested until fully ripe – when the fruits have turned from green to grey. Cut the plants and leave them on the ground for a day or two to ripen completely. Shake out the seeds and store.

Uses The seeds are used as flavouring for bread, curry, pickles and sauces. The leaves can be chopped like parsley to be used as a garnish and flavouring.

Coriander

Costmary

COSTMARY, ALECOST

Chrysanthemum balsamita

A medium-sized perennial that dies down each winter. The leaves have a scent of mint and the flavour of lemon. Costmary will not propagate by seed, but division of its extensive and invasive root system in spring will ensure a generous supply of plants that will grow in any sunny, well-drained soil.

Harvesting Pick fresh leaves as required.

Uses Use fresh leaves in brewing beer, in stuffings and tisanes.

Cotton lavender

COTTON LAVENDER

Santolina chamaecyparissus

A shrubby perennial that grows up to 60cm (2ft) in height. It has silver-grey leaves and yellow flowers. Cotton lavender requires a sunny position but is happy in most soils. Propagate by stem cuttings in summer or layering older stems, and by root division in spring. Clip back plants in spring to keep them in shape and, if only foliage is required, again in summer.

Uses Cotton lavender makes a good edging hedge and has strongly scented leaves.

CUMIN

Cuminum cyminum

A half-hardy annual that grows to a height of 15cm (6in). It has feathery foliage and tiny insignificant white or mauve flowers. Sow seeds under glass in early spring or directly into the garden in a sunny position as soon as the danger of frost has passed. Thin seedlings to 10cm (4in) apart. Cumin will only produce seeds if the summer is long and hot.

Harvesting Cut the stems before the seeds have ripened fully and hang them up to dry. The seeds only develop their full flavour when completely dry.

Uses Ground or used whole, the seeds add a pungent flavour to meat dishes and curries.

CURRY PLANT

Helichrysum angustifolium

A shrubby perennial that grows to a height of 45cm (18in) with silver foliage and golden-brown flowers in summer. Grow in well-drained soil in a sunny and sheltered position – the curry plant is only just hardy. Propagate by stem cuttings in late summer, but protect the new cuttings from any danger of frost.

Harvesting Pick fresh leaves throughout summer and cut sprays for drying before flowers have fully opened.

Uses The distinctive curry flavour of the chopped leaves enhances sauces, fish, meat and egg dishes.

DILL

Anethum graveolens

A sharply aromatic feathery annual grown for its leaves and seeds, dill will grow up to 90cm (3ft) in height. It prefers a sunny well-drained site, but avoid planting near fennel as cross-pollination may occur. Sow seeds in spring and in succession throughout summer. Thin seedlings to 23cm (9in) apart.

Harvesting Pick leaves as required and leaves for drying just before flowering. Allow seeds to ripen on the plant, shake out and store.

Uses Both leaves and seeds are used to flavour a wide variety of dishes, vinegar and pickles.

ELECAMPANE
Inula helenium
A tall decorative perennial reaching a height of 2m (7ft). It has large leaves and flowers that may reach 10cm (4in) across. The perfect background plant for the herb garden, elecampane will grow in sun or partial shade on almost any moist soil. Sow seeds in spring or propagate by root division in spring or autumn. Renew plants every three or four years.
Harvesting Lift roots in autumn.
Uses Mainly ornamental, but the bitter aromatic root is sometimes used to flavour liqueurs or confectionery.

FENNEL
Foeniculum vulgare
A tall perennial reaching a height of 1.5m (5ft) or more. Its fine feathery foliage and umbels of yellow flowers make it an attractive decorative plant for the garden. Sow seeds in shallow drills in spring and thin the plants to 40cm (16in) apart. Do not plant near dill as cross-pollination may occur. In autumn cut down plants to within 10cm (4in) from ground-level.
Harvesting Pick leaves as required. Gather flowerheads in autumn before they are completely ripe and dry slowly on paper. When ripe, shake off the seeds and store.
Uses Good with fish and in marinades, soups, sauces and salads.

FENUGREEK
Trigonella foenum-graecum
A hardy annual that is grown for its leaves and seeds. It resembles clover and grows to a height of 60cm (2ft). Heavily scented cream flowers appear in summer and develop into large pods of seeds. Sow seeds in a sunny, well-drained position in spring, when frost is not a threat.
Harvesting Pick leaves as required. When the plant has produced seed and the pods are brown, uproot the whole plant and dry. Remove the dry seeds from the pods and store in an airtight container.
Uses Leaves can be used in salads. The seeds are usually lightly roasted and ground and then added to curry powders, pickles and chutneys.

GAS PLANT
Dictamnus albus
A bushy perennial that reaches a height of 60cm (2ft). It has dark green shiny leaves and long spikes of delicate white flowers. The gas plant will grow in partial shade but prefers full sun and a light, well-drained soil. Either acquire young plants or propagate by seed sown 1m (3ft) apart in their permanent position.
Uses Grown as an ornamental for its lemon-scented leaves and attractive flowers. It takes its common name from the fact that in hot dry weather it produces an oily vapour that can burst into flame if lit.

HAMBURG PARSLEY
Petroselinum tuberosum
This variety of parsley is grown for its roots which are cooked and eaten like parsnips. The leaves can be used for flavouring, in the same way as ordinary parsley, but they lack flavour. Sow seeds outdoors in spring and thin them to 25cm (10in) apart when they are large enough to handle.
Harvesting Lift the roots from early autumn onwards.
Uses Use roots as a pot vegetable and the leaves for flavouring.

HOREHOUND
Marrubium vulgare

Fenugreek

Gas plant

A hardy perennial growing to a height of 60cm (2ft). It has round, wrinkled leaves and circles of white flowers along the stem. Horehound will grow in any soil and can tolerate partial shade. Sow seeds in spring and thin plants to 25cm (10in) when they are large enough to handle. Root division in spring or autumn will thereafter provide a good supply of plants.
Uses Mainly ornamental, but horehound was once used as an excellent remedy for coughs.

HORSERADISH

Cochlearia armoracia

A hardy perennial grown for its roots. With so much wild horseradish growing at the side of the road it may not seem worthwhile giving up garden space to this plant. But garden-grown horseradish has larger roots with a much stronger flavour. Plant crowns in deep, rich moist soil in spring, leaving 30cm (12in) between each plant. Pick off flowers as they

Horseradish

appear. Replace the bed each year, otherwise the plants may take over.
Harvesting Lift roots in autumn and store small roots in sand for planting next spring.
Uses To make horseradish sauce.
NB: leaves and stems are poisonous.

Hyssop

Lavender

HYSSOP

Hyssopus officinalis

A perennial sub-shrub with bright blue, pink or white flowers in summer. Ideal for a low hedge border to the herb garden. It grows 60cm (2ft) tall and is suitable for most positions in the garden, but prefers a sunny place and a light soil. Sow seeds in spring and plant out seedlings to 45cm (1½ft). Take cuttings or divide the roots in spring or autumn.

Harvesting Collect the leaves as the flowers are beginning to bloom.

Uses The leaves have a slightly bitter, minty flavour and can be added to salads, soups and meat, especially pork. Use sparingly as the flavour is very strong.

LADY'S MANTLE

Alchemilla vulgaris

A hardy perennial that grows to 30cm (12in) in height and forms a good ground cover. It has pleated fan-like leaves and clusters of small yellow flowers. Lady's mantle will grow in shade and grow well in any well-drained soil. Sow seeds under glass and transfer them to the garden in late-spring. Alternatively, propagate by root division in spring, placing plants 15cm (6in) apart.

Harvesting Pick fresh leaves as required.

Uses Mainly ornamental, although the fresh leaves can be used for a tisane.

LAVENDER

Lavandula officinalis

A perennial sub-shrub with grey-green needle-like foliage and spikes of tiny purple flowers. It will grow in poor soil but needs a sunny position. Lavender does not grow well from seed so either buy young plants or take green cuttings in summer. Place plants about 30cm (1ft) apart.

Clip over the bush after flowering to keep it a good shape, but do not cut into old wood. Give light clipping in spring to encourage growth at the base of the plant. Replace plants every five or six years.
Harvesting Cut flower spikes as they come into flower and dry in the dark to keep the colour.
Uses Lavender has no culinary use and is grown as an ornamental for the scent of its flowers and its ability to attract bees.

LEMON BALM

Melissa officinalis
A hardy perennial growing to a height of 1.2m (4ft) with deep green leaves that smell strongly of lemon. It grows in almost any soil but prefers a sunny position. The roots are invasive, so unless you want vast quantities of leaves, restrict the roots by planting it in a bottomless bucket or an old pot. Sow seeds in spring or propagate by root division in spring or autumn. Pinch out flowers for maximum leaf production.

Lemon balm

Harvesting Pick fresh leaves as required. Cut stems at the end of summer and hang them up to dry.
Uses The lemon flavour complements stewed fruit, fish and poultry. The dried leaves make a refreshing tisane.

LEMON VERBENA

Aloysia triphylla
A tender perennial that can grow to more than 3m (10ft). It has long pointed leaves and small mauve flowers that appear in late summer. To propagate lemon verbena take stem cuttings in late spring or early summer and plant them in well-drained soil in a sunny, sheltered position. Protect from frost in winter.
Harvesting Collect leaves as they are shed from the plant in autumn.
Uses Use fresh in lemon sauces, salads and fruit dishes. Added to the tea-pot a few leaves transform ordinary tea. It can also be made into a tisane with mint.

LOVAGE

Levisticum officinale
A giant perennial, growing to about 2m (6ft) tall with umbels of yellowish flowers in late summer. Lovage prefers a rich, moist soil and will tolerate semi-shade. Sow seeds in spring or propagate by root division in spring or autumn. Space plants about 45cm (1½ft) apart. Unless more seed is required cut the flowerheads to encourage leaf growth.
Harvesting Pick fresh leaves as required. Drying is difficult and takes up to five days. Gather seeds as they ripen.
Uses Both leaves and seeds will enrich salads, soups, sauces and stews. The celery-like flavour is strong, so use with discretion.

MARIGOLD
Calendula officinalis
One of the easiest and most rewarding of flowers. An annual with flowers ranging in colour from yellow to deep orange, they are a welcome addition to any garden or window box. Marigold will self-seed freely, but to keep them within bounds sow seeds in spring or autumn.
Harvesting Pick fresh flowers as required or dry petals in the dark so they retain their colour.
Uses The petals can be substituted for saffron in cooking. They produce the same colour, but not the flavour. Also add to salads and omelettes.

MARJORAM
Origanum spp
There are many different varieties of *Origanum,* each with the same characteristic flavour and scent. All require light, well-drained slightly acid soil and full sun. Propagate by cuttings, seed and root division in spring and autumn. The three best known varieties are:

Wild marjoram

Sweet Marjoram
O. marjorana
Although a perennial it is best grown as an annual. Do not sow outdoors until the soil has warmed up, perhaps as late as the end of May. It can be sown earlier in heat and set out in a warm sheltered bed. Protect from frost.

Pot Marjoram
O. onites
Green-stemmed and usually white-flowered, it can be grown in a pot indoors for use in winter.

Wild marjoram, oregano
O. vulgare
This has reddish stems and, usually, purple flowers. It grows wild on the limestone hills of Britain where it has a milder flavour than pot marjoram. Grown in hot Mediterranean climates, however, it has a strong pungent taste and is known as oregano.
Harvesting Pick fresh leaves and flowers as required. All varieties dry well and their flavour becomes stronger. Always dry in the dark.
Uses A wide range of uses and one of the most versatile of culinary herbs.

MINTS
Mentha spp
There are more than 40 varieties of mint, of which a few – all perennials – are well-known and widely grown. Propagate by root division in spring and autumn. Mints are rampant and can soon take over a herb garden. Control spreading by planting in a clay pot or in a bottomless old bucket. The most common varieties of mint are:

Peppermint

Spearmint

Peppermint

M. piperita

Grows up to 60cm (2ft) tall with longish pointed leaves and purple flowers in autumn. Oil from this plant is used to give peppermint flavour to confectionery.

Applemint

M. rotundifolia

Up to 90cm (3ft) in height with round furry leaves and purplish-white flowers in autumn. Many people prefer the flavour to spearmint.

Spearmint

M. spicata

The best-known of mints, and the one generally used for mint sauce. It grows up to 60cm (2ft) tall and has pointed leaves and purplish flowers in autumn.

Harvesting Pick fresh leaves as required and cut for drying when the flowers are in bud. Dry in the dark.

Uses Mint sauce or jelly for roast lamb, and to add flavour to boiled potatoes and carrots. Pleasant fresh in salads and fruit drinks. The dried leaves make a refreshing tea.

Applemint

MUGWORT
Artemisia vulgaris
A woody-stemmed perennial growing to 60cm (2ft) in height. Buy young plants for planting in late spring in well-drained soil and in a sunny position. Mugwort has dark green spiky leaves and small reddish-brown flowers.
Harvesting Cut shoots during mid- and late-summer. Discard the leaves and stems and keep the buds.
Uses The buds can be used as seasoning. The leaves can be chopped and added to fatty meats such as pork and goose.

PARSLEY
Petroselinum crispum
The best-known and most widely used of herbs, parsley is a biennial usually grown as an annual. Most varieties have curly leaves but some varieties have flat leaves, which have a stronger flavour but are coarser. Sow seeds in spring and in succession throughout summer. Seeds are slow to germinate and soaking them for 24 hours before sowing may speed up the process. Thin the plants to 8cm (3in), and then to 20cm (8in) so they do not quite touch each other when mature. Protect from frosts.
Harvesting Pick fresh leaves as required.
Uses There are few dishes that parsley does not improve.

PENNYROYAL
Mentha pulegium
A tiny creeping member of the mint family that only grows to a height of 15cm (6in) and produces purple flowers in autumn. Grow in almost any position as long as the soil is fairly rich. Propagate by root division.
Uses An ornamental mint that can be used to form an aromatic lawn.

Mugwort

Parsley

PURSLANE

Portulaca oleracea

A sprawling annual that reaches a height of 15cm (6in) with rosettes of fleshy leaves and yellow flowers. Sow seeds in spring, when the danger of frost has passed, in well-drained soil and a sunny position. Thin plants to 15cm (6in) when large enough to handle.

Harvesting Pick young leaves for using fresh or drying as required. Pick shoots when they are 8cm (3in) in length.

Uses Young leaves can be used in salads, older leaves are coarser and should be cooked like spinach. Cook the shoots and use as vegetables.

ROSEMARY

Rosmarinus officinalis

An evergreen perennial shrub that reaches a height of 90cm (3ft). The aromatic leaves are needle-shaped and the flowers pale blue. Grow in a well-drained, preferably sandy soil in a sheltered spot. Propagate by heel-cuttings in spring or by root division in spring or autumn. Young plants may need to be protected from frost.

Harvesting Pick fresh leaves and flowers as required and cut shoots for drying in summer.

Uses Rosemary adds flavour to roast meats, especially lamb, veal and chicken. Excellent for stuffings and marinades.

RUE

Ruta graveolens

A hardy evergreen shrub with blue-green leaves and yellow flowers in summer. It grows to a height of 60cm (2ft) in almost any soil, but prefers a sunny position. Rue will seed itself or you can take cuttings in early summer. Keep plants about 30cm (1ft) apart. Clipping over the plant every other spring will encourage bushy growth.

Rue

Rosemary

Harvesting Pick leaves as required.

Uses Principally a decorative plant, but the leaves can be used in very small quantities to flavour salad dressings.

Beware: large quantities of rue can be poisonous and many people are allergic to it.

SAGE
Salvia officinalis
A fast-spreading perennial shrub that grows to a height of about 60cm (2ft). It has grey-green hairy leaves and spikes of purple flowers. Sage will grow almost anywhere, but prefers sun and dislikes too much moisture. Propagate by seed sown in spring, or by cuttings, or by pegging down runners that can be moved when they have rooted. Keep plants about 40cm (16in) apart. Prune to keep in shape and renew plants every four years as they become thin and woody.
Harvesting Pick leaves as required, but they are at their best before flowering. Dry very slowly.
Uses Its best-known use is in sage and onion stuffing, but it goes well with all rich fatty meats such as pork and duck.

Sage

SALAD BURNET
Sanguisorba minor
This perennial herb grows to a height of 60cm (2ft) and has rosettes of leaves and pink or white flowers. Sow seeds in spring in rows 30cm (1ft) apart – once established it will seed itself. Salad burnet will grow in almost any soil and is extremely hardy, producing green leaves all year round. Pinch out flowers if you want to use the leaves regularly.
Harvesting Pick leaves as required.
Uses The cucumber-flavoured leaves add flavour to cool drinks, salads and sauces. Young leaves have a more delicate taste.

SAVORY
Satureja spp
An aromatic herb that resembles a long-leaved thyme. Two different varieties are grown:

Summer Savory
S. hortensis
A bushy annual that grows to a height of 45cm (1½ft) and has pink flowers in late summer. Sow in a sunny position in early summer.
Harvesting Cut sprigs before flowering, for use fresh or for drying.
Uses Traditionally used in bean dishes.

Winter Savory
S. montana
A hardy dwarf evergreen perennial that grows to a height of 45cm (1½ft) and bears white or blue flowers. Sow seeds in late-spring and thin to 22cm (6-8in) apart. It may be necessary to protect the plant from heavy frosts.
Harvesting Pick leaves as required throughout the year.
Uses Traditionally used in bean dishes.

Winter savory

SORREL

Rumex scutatus

A cross between a herb and a leaf vegetable. Sorrel has arrow-shaped leaves and grows to a height of 60cm (2ft). It prefers a well-drained slightly acid soil but will tolerate partial shade. Sow seed in spring or divide roots in spring or autumn. Keep plants about 30cm (12in) apart. Leaf growth can be encouraged by removing flowering stems; this also keeps the leaves tender.

Harvesting Pick fresh leaves as required.

Uses Young tender leaves can be used in salads, but older leaves should be treated like spinach and used in soups as a puréed vegetable.

Sorrel

SOUTHERNWOOD, LAD'S LOVE

Artemisia abrotanum

Beware: never eat the leaves of this plant as they are poisonous. Originally grown in herb gardens to keep witches out, this small perennial shrub has woody stems and feathery grey-green leaves covered in down. Plant in late autumn or early spring in a sunny, light, well-drained soil, leaving 38cm (15in) between each plant. Propagate by cuttings in spring.

Harvesting Cut branches at end of summer and dry.

Uses Mostly decorative, it can be used in small amounts in pot-pourri. The dried branches act as a moth repellent if put in cupboards.

Southernwood

SWEET CICELY

Myrrhis odorata

A decorative perennial that takes several years to reach its full height of 1.5m (5ft). It has feathery leaves and umbels of white flowers. Sweet cicely will seed itself freely, and take over the garden, but sow seeds in spring in a well-drained, but rich soil, in partial shade. Once plants are established propagate by root division in spring or autumn.

Harvesting Pick leaves as required and leaves for drying in spring.

Uses The sweet taste and smell is rather like aniseed. Chopped leaves can be added to salads or fruit. The roots can be cooked as a vegetable.

TARRAGON

Artemisia dracunculus

There are two varieties of tarragon, Russian (*A. dracunculoides*) and French (*A. dracunculus*). Both are shrubby perennials that grow to a height of 1m (3ft), but the French variety (also called estragon) has a far superior taste. Tarragon requires full sun and light, well-drained soil. Propagation is by root division or cuttings planted in spring when the danger of frost has passed. Plant them 45-60cm (1½-2ft) apart as the root system is extensive. French tarragon deteriorates after about four years and plants must be divided and replanted or replaced.

Harvesting Use fresh leaves as required throughout summer and autumn. Cut stems for drying or freezing in mid-summer.

Uses A wide range of culinary uses.

Sweet cicely (below) and tarragon (right)

TANSY
Tanacetum vulgare
A perennial herb growing to a height of 90cm (3ft). It is an extremely attractive ornamental with aromatic, dark green ferny leaves and clusters of button-like yellow flowers. Sow seed in spring in any soil in a sunny position, or propagate by root division in spring or autumn. Be careful – tansy spreads very quickly.
Harvesting Pick leaves as required.
Uses Mainly ornamental. The leaves were traditionally used to flavour tansy cakes eaten at Easter.

THYME
Thymus spp
A fast spreading perennial herb with a strong scent. Grow in full sun. Thyme can be propagated by seed, root division, heel cuttings or by pegging down branches and severing them when roots have formed. Trim tops after flowering and protect from severe frost. Replant every three or four years when the plants become straggly. There are several culinary varieties of thyme, including the following,

Tansy

Common thyme

Lemon thyme

Woad

Common Thyme
T. vulgaris
A low bush growing to a height of 30cm (1ft).
Harvesting Pick leaves fresh up to, and during, flowering time. Dries well.
Uses Adds flavour to stews, poultry, sausages and game.

Lemon Thyme
T. citriodorus
A creeping perennial growing to a height of only 15cm (6in).
Harvesting The same as common thyme.
Uses Good with fish or fruit dishes.

VERVAIN
Verbena officinalis
A pretty perennial plant with pointed leaves and spikes of purple flowers. Propagate by cuttings, root division or seed sown in spring. Vervain needs a rich well-drained soil in a sunny position.
Harvesting Cut sprigs for using fresh or for drying in summer before the flowers open.
Uses Mainly ornamental although a tisane can be made from the leaves.

WOAD
Isatis tinctoria
A hardy biennial with blue-green leaves and yellow flowers that grow to a height of up to 1.2m (4ft). Sow seeds in full-sun or partial shade in late summer, and the following spring thin them to 30cm (1ft) apart.
Uses Ornamental – the leaves yield a blue dye that was used by Ancient Britons to paint their bodies.

WOODRUFF
Asperula odorata
A low-growing carpeting perennial that requires a humus-rich, damp shady woodland site. The ruff-like leaves give off a scent like new-mown hay. Seeds take a long time to germinate so plant young plants 20cm (8in) apart in spring.
Harvesting Pick fresh leaves as required. The leaves develop their strongest scent when first picked and beginning to dry.
Uses Add leaves to white wine and apple juice. They can also be used for a tisane.

Woodruff

WORMWOOD
Artemisia absinthium
A hardy perennial shrub that grows to a height of 90cm (3ft). Wormwood thrives in almost any soil in sun or partial shade. Sow seeds in autumn or propagate by stem cuttings or root division. Set plants about 60cm (2ft) apart.
Uses Wormwood is grown in the herb or flower garden as an ornamental. It is extremely bitter and used to flavour vermouth and absinthe, but taken in quantity it is extremely dangerous to eat as it has a narcotic effect.

HERB GARDEN PLANNER

	C	c	F	T	B	O	S
ANGELICA		■	■	■		■	■
ANISE		■	■	■	■		
ANISE HYSSOP			■		■		■
BASIL	■		■			■	
BAY	■		■			■	■
BERGAMOT			■	■	■	■	
BORAGE		■			■		
CARAWAY		■					
CATMINT			■	■	■	■	■
CHAMOMILE, ROMAN			■	■			
CHAMOMILE, TRUE			■	■			
CHERVIL		■				■	
CHIVES	■					■	■
CLARY		■	■				
COMFREY		■				■	■
CORIANDER		■					
COSTMARY		■	■				
COTTON LAVENDER			■			■	
CUMIN		■	■				
CURRY PLANT		■	■				
DILL	■						
ELECAMPANE		■				■	■
FENNEL	■					■	
FENUGREEK		■	■				
GAS PLANT			■			■	
HAMBURG PARSLEY		■					
HOREHOUND			■	■	■		■
HORSERADISH		■					■
HYSSOP		■	■			■	■
LADY'S MANTLE		■				■	■
LAVENDER			■		■	■	

KEY TO SYMBOLS

- **C** Major culinary use
- **c** Culinary use
- **F** Fragrant
- **T** Used for making herbal teas
- **B** Attractive to bees
- **S** Will tolerate partial shade
- **O** Ornamental

	C	c	F	T	B	O	S
LEMON BALM		■	■	■			
LEMON VERBENA		■	■			■	
LOVAGE		■					■
MARIGOLD		■				■	
MARJORAM, SWEET	■						
POT	■						
OREGANO	■						
MINTS, APPLEMINT	■		■				■
PEPPERMINT	■		■				■
SPEARMINT	■		■	■			■
MUGWORT		■				■	
PARSLEY	■						
PENNYROYAL			■			■	■
PURSLANE		■				■	
ROSEMARY	■		■		■	■	
RUE		■	■			■	
SAGE	■	■				■	
SALAD BURNET		■	■			■	
SAVORY, SUMMER		■				■	
WINTER		■				■	
SORREL		■					■
SOUTHERNWOOD						■	
SWEET CICELY		■	■		■	■	■
TARRAGON	■						
TANSY		■				■	■
THYME, COMMON	■		■			■	
LEMON	■		■			■	
VERVAIN			■	■			■
WOAD						■	■
WOODRUFF		■	■				■
WORMWOOD						■	

INDEX AND ACKNOWLEDGEMENTS

Picture Credits

Ken Beckett: 4/5, 14, 16, 17(t), 24(b), 30(t), 33(tr), 40, 42(l), 44(bl).
Iris Hardwick Library: 13, 21.
Peter Myers: 18/9.
David Russell: 24(t), 25(t,b), 26(t,b), 27, 29(t,b), 30(b), 31, 33(tl,b), 34(t), 35, 36, 37(t,bl,br), 38(t,b), 39(t,b), 41, 42(r), 43(t,b), 44(tl,r), 45.
Harry Smith Horticultural Photographic Collection: 6/7, 15, 17(b), 20, 22/3, 34(b), 44(cl).
George Wright: 19.

Artwork by

Richard Prideaux & Steve Sandilands